My Grandbaby My Love

Written By:
Delemesa Mack Taylor

Illustrated By:
Nadeem CH

You are my grandbaby and
I love you. You are so perfect and
bring me joy through and through.

The smile on your face and the light in your eyes make my heart leap with joy when you are nearby.

A new life and a new love what a sweet gift you are.

I could never have imagined you my little shooting star.

Your laugh, your cry, your soft gentle touch,

All a part of you my grandbaby and
I love you so much.

Today and always, I'm grateful

my special love you'll be.

The joy you have brought to my world is so heavenly.

I love holding your hand and kissing your feet. When I look in your eyes my heart skips a beat.

You are my grandbaby and such a beautiful soul. I can't wait to get to know you and although I'm getting old,

I know that you're truly a gift from above,
To fill my remaining days with joy my grandbaby, my love.

You are my grandbaby and I love you.

There's nothing else I'd rather do, than to love and cherish you and create fond memories.

My grandbaby, my love you forever will be.

Milton Keynes UK
Ingram Content Group UK Ltd.
UKHW051517131124
451074UK00009B/125